Resilient Whispers

Poems of Survival and Strength

Kathryn A. Warrington

BookLeaf Publishing

India | USA | UK

Dedication

To the perilous people who have survived
everything sent to break them.

Acknowledgment

To all those who helped, supported, and listened to my rantings day after day while I struggled to make it through.

Preface

After living in a horror story, I always knew I was strong, but I never knew how strong I had to be to survive. This is a path of healing and perseverance. This is my journey, the one that made me into a survivor, and no one can take that away.

Stone

The tear fell silent,
And sparkling on her cheek;
Hardened, turned to stone.

Starved

Everything taken from me.
Food while I was eating,
Money I earned.
Sleep I needed.
Happiness I yearned for.
My life, blow by blow, hit by hit, word by word,
All taken from me,
And now I take everything back.

Gone

A heart aches and bleeds,
Words and feelings etched in time,
Taken, never to return.

Do you think

Do you think he cares what he did?
Think he feels what I felt?
The fear, the desperation, the anger.
Fighting to stay and fighting to go.
Do you think he cares what he did?
The longing, the ache, the terror.
Giving up and letting go.

Life

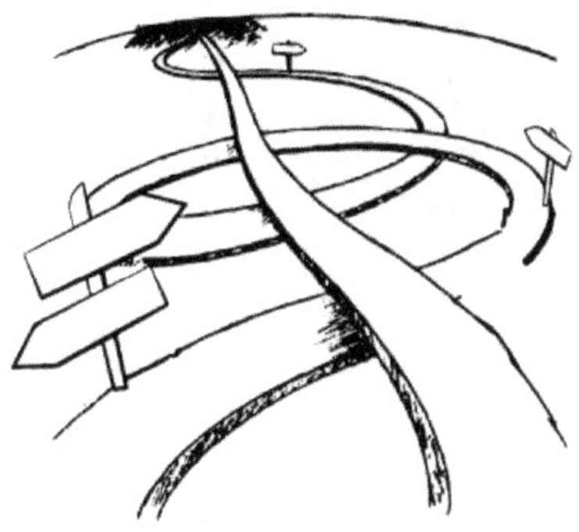

Life begins with birth and ends with death,
Everything in between is a path on which we
learn.
A single choice can make life turn.
Vicarious events make a path we walk,
Every thought shapes the way we talk.

Lies

Till the road runs dry,
You try to cover up all his lies,
But you can't save him.
He did this to himself, and now he is the only
one who will pay.
Say goodbye; he made his own future,
Now he cries.

Halfway

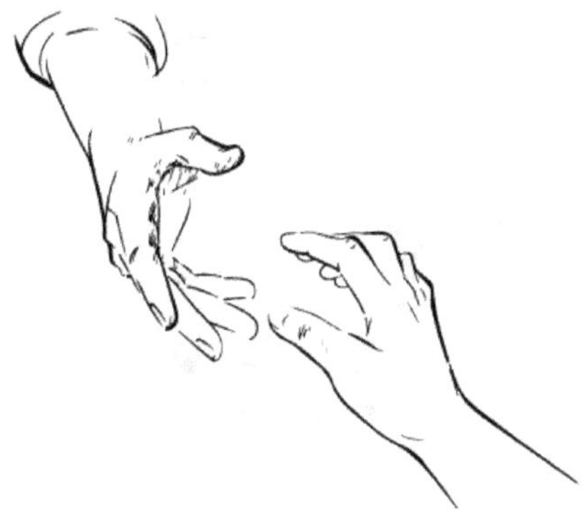

Halfway between people and halfway
promises.
In and out, back and forth,
Forever in my mind, long lost but not
forgotten.
Searching for every thought,
Every memory and every sound, to bring you
back.

Empty

Thoughtless encounters,
Written on the steps of hope.
Memories stuck in space and time.

Dark

Silence greeted her.
Deafening in the night;
Burning the darkness.

Loneliness

There's something to be said when you feel
lonely, even when around other people.
Like a sledgehammer in your mind, telling
you that you're not good enough.
That you will never make it,
That you're weak,
Inept at life.
The depression, it creeps in like that.
Like a sick, twisted cloud of self-doubt.
Like a downpour that never stops, till
someone comes to you with an umbrella,
To help build you up, to shield you from that
storm,
But what if no one ever comes?

Death

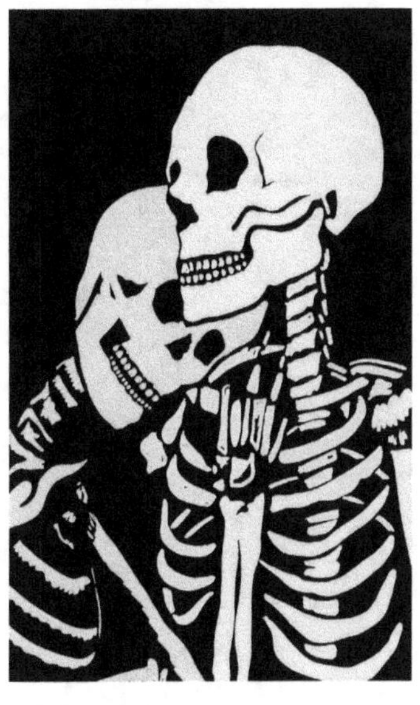

Death seemed like a good escape,
Creeping away in the night
Fading away till there is nothing left.

Early

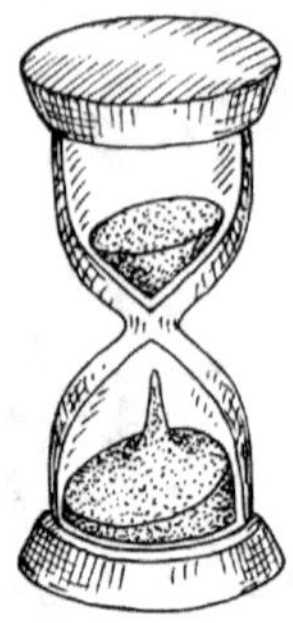

She sat on the steps.
A new journey creeping into the timeline,
It was now her time to shine.

Transcending

Staring at the sky,
Black with night and sprinkled with stars.
She began the journey with a sigh.
A wishful hope.

Fake

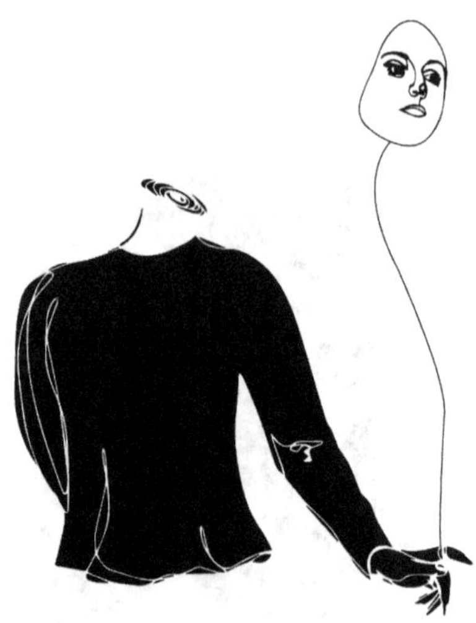

I want you to see something real,
I want you to feel real raw emotion and hear
sounds to fill the silent air,
I want the universe to stop and stare,
To take in the rush like a final meal,
Before your neck meets the steel.

Perilous

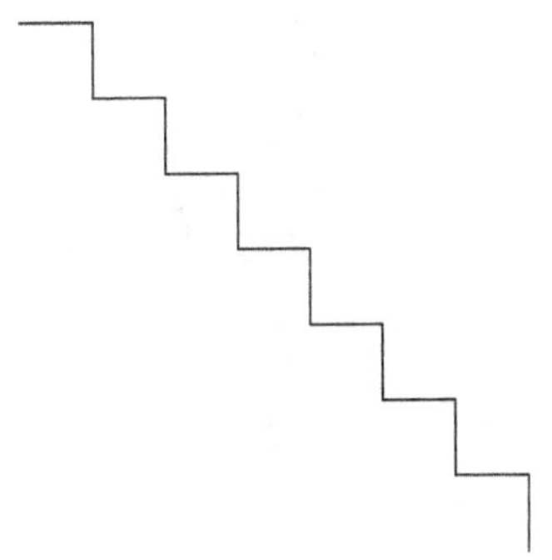

She was perilously perplexed,
Hanging on the edge of tomorrow.
Making sluggish steps to the finish line,
Never letting go of her vibrant soul.

Furious

The grim thoughts compounded.
A swift anger formed.
Furiously challenging,
Starving the sober mind.

Drive

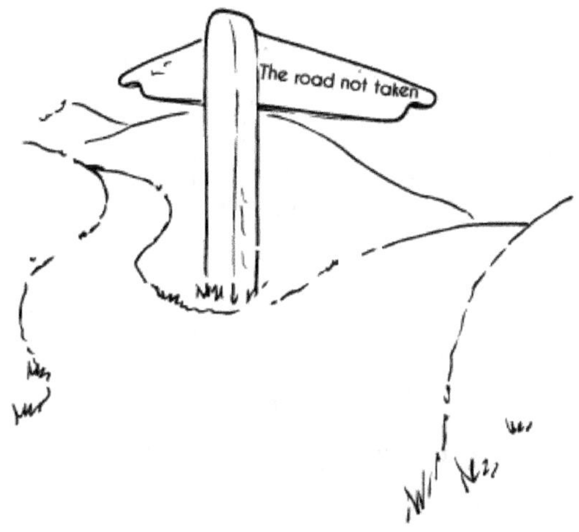

Shiny, black, and unforgiving,
Melting away beneath me.
A release into the night.
Lifting away all my worries.
Loving my soul with asphalt tenderness.
Caressing my worries in a passing shadow.

Chaos

Opening the door to chaos,
A song leads the way.
Memories causing flames to erupt,
A cold heat burning the day.

Thankful

Waking up from a nightmare,
Thankful for every day.
Understanding that I am worth more,
Thankful for inner strength.

Fighting

She's fighting every day,
For truth, in a battle against the lies.
The shade thrown over so many eyes,
Fighting to show the truth,
Shining a light in the darkness,
Under the sweet, crushing veil, she sighs.

Anger To Strength

In anger, strength worms its way in,
Festering till it spills out of lips that were
sewn shut.
Seeping through the cement left by the past,
Disintegrating generations and building
monuments of power.